Rome

EVERGREEN is an imprint of TASCHEN GmbH

© for this edition: 2001 TASCHEN GmbH
Hohenzollernring 53, D–50672 Köln
© 2000 Editions du Chêne – Hachette Livre – Rome
Under the direction of Michel Buntz
Text: Denis Montagnon
Photographs: Benoît Roland
Layout: Roger Donadini
Map and illustrations: Jean-Michel Kirsch
Editor: Corinne Fossey
Cover design: Angelika Taschen, Cologne

Translated by Ian West
In association with First Edition Translations Ltd, Cambridge
Realisation of the English edition by First Edition Translations Ltd, Cambridge

Printed in Italy
ISBN 3-8228-5870-6

Rome

Text
DENIS MONTAGNON

Photographs
BENOÎT ROLAND

EVERGREEN

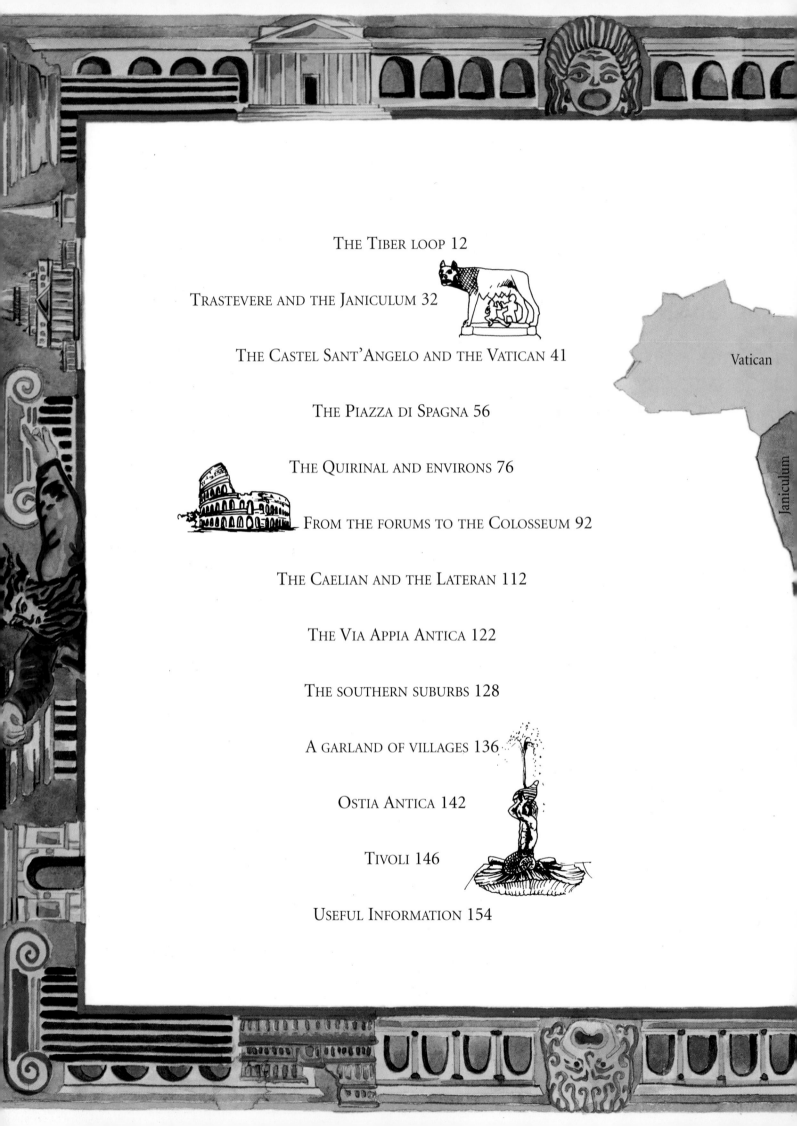

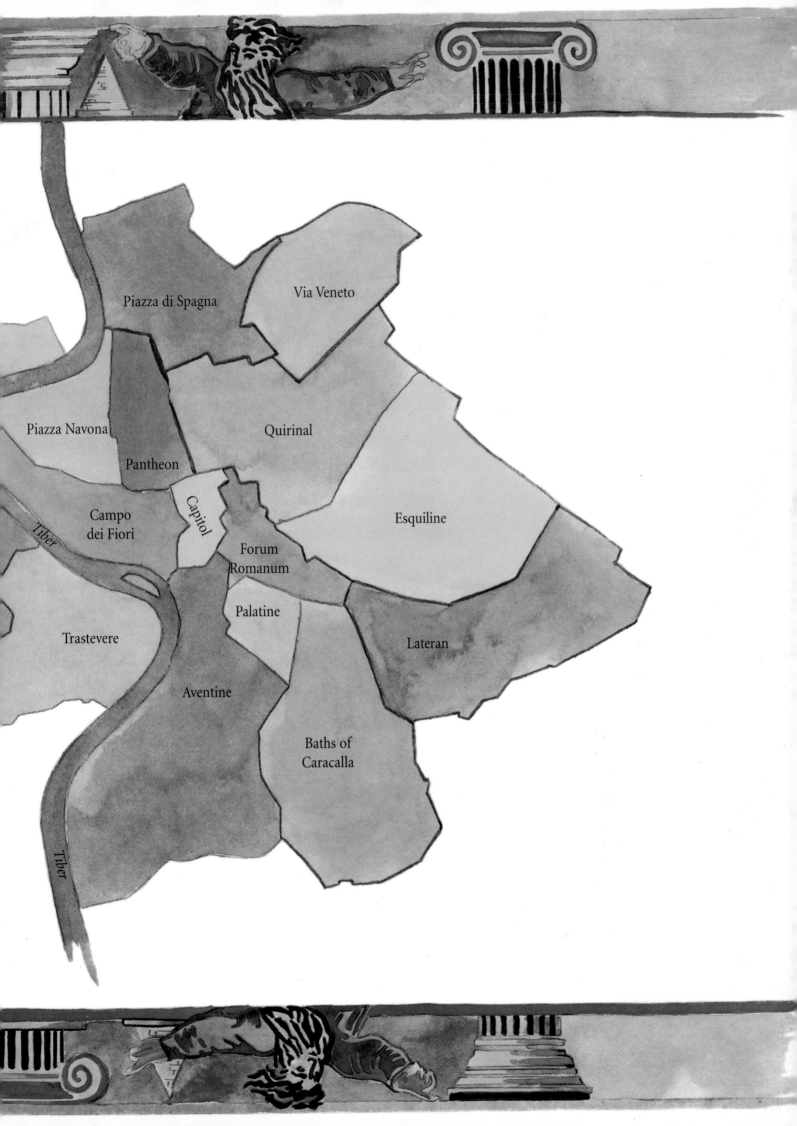

Piazza di Spagna

Via Veneto

Piazza Navona

Quirinal

Pantheon

Capitol

Campo
dei Fiori

Esquiline

Tiber

Forum
Romanum

Palatine

Trastevere

Lateran

Aventine

Baths of
Caracalla

Tiber

An inexhaustible store of treasures, an eternity of dazzling moments…
This is how Rome has always struck its visitors. Fashioned by the
passage of centuries, the city magically blends relics of Antiquity, narrow
medieval streets, and airy, spacious quarters befitting a young and thriving capital.

Legendary origins

Fleeing from Troy, Aeneas landed at Ostia and made his home in Latium. From
the love affairs of Mars with the distant descendant of Venus' son, the Vestal
Rhea Silvia, were born two children whom their usurping uncle – the king of
Alba Longa – soon attempted to remove by casting them adrift on the River
Tiber. We all know the rest of the story. Romulus and Remus, adopted by a she-
wolf at the foot of the Palatine, founded Rome in 753 BC. Romulus ploughed a
furrow marking the sacred boundary. His brother jokingly leapt over it;
Romulus killed him and became sole master of the Latins.

Ancient Rome

Centuries of almost uninterrupted expansion followed. After the Etruscan
interlude, Rome established its authority first on the Italian mainland, then,
under the Republic, as a Mediterranean power (509–27 BC). Under the Empire
(27 BC to the fourth century AD), its influence extended from the Atlantic to
the Persian Gulf and the Caspian Sea.

So vast an empire demanded a worthy capital. To the sanctuary of the Capitol
dominating the Forum Romanum were added temples, patrician mansions,
and a whole variety of utilitarian buildings to fulfil the needs of a population
which, in the first century BC, exceeded a million. The greatest of the emperor-
builders flourished in the eras of the Julio-Claudians (27 BC–AD 68), the
Flavians (69–96), and the Antonines (96–192), at the height of the Pax Romana.
It is to them that Rome owes the Pantheon, the Colosseum, Trajan's Column,
and Hadrian's Villa at Tivoli.

Christian Rome

In 312, the Emperor Constantine (306–337) ordered an end to the persecution of Christians. As the catacombs were gradually abandoned, huge basilicas arose above the tombs of the Apostles and the earliest successors of Peter: San Paolo fuori le mura, the first St Peter's, San Clemente... The popes took up residence in a palace close to St John Lateran, the first sanctuary of the city dedicated to Christ; they were to remain there till their departure for Avignon at the start of the fourteenth century. After the barbarian invasions, and the deposition of the last Roman emperor in 476, it was the papacy that assured the city's survival. Under the aegis of Charlemagne, Rome rose from its ruins – only to be battered by further storms in the Middle Ages as popes, emperors, and nobility waged a relentless struggle for power. Though the city's life resumed little by little, it was mainly confined to the loop of the Tiber and Trastevere, on the left bank. Travellers found sheep grazing amid the remains of the Capitol, the Palatine and the Esquiline in scenes of near desolation.

Rome during the Renaissance and the Baroque

The ending of the Great Schism in 1417 saw the seat of the papacy restored definitively from Avignon to Rome, but to a Rome that was disease ridden, depopulated, and disreputable. Even the Lateran Palace was in ashes! Secure in their new authority, the popes entered upon a long series of reconstructions which was to last more than two centuries. Sixtus IV (1471–1484), the first great papal builder, mapped out new streets in the ancient quarter of the Campus Martius. He added more bridges, oversaw the construction of the Sistine Chapel in his new Vatican Palace, and renovated numerous churches. Julius II (1503–1513) recruited the finest artists of his time to work on the second St Peter's. At the end of the sixteenth century, Sixtus V (1585–1590) founded another series of churches. He erected obelisks in public squares and remodelled the district of the Quirinal, leaving a legacy of city planning admired throughout the continent.

Following pages: One of the grandest surviving monuments of Antiquity, the Colosseum, is also an emblem of the city of the seven hills. 'Rome will last as long as the Colosseum. When the Colosseum falls, Rome will fall, and the whole world with her': quoted by the Venerable Bede (673–735).

The seventeenth century ushered in the age of the Baroque, when the grand redesign of the papal city reached its climax. Nothing was too magnificent to recapture the primacy of Rome, which had suffered so severely under the Reformation and through the sack of the city in 1527. The pontificates of Urban VIII (1623–1644) and Innocent X (1644–1655) witnessed the completion of St Peter's Basilica and the laying out of the famous Piazza Navona by the great architect and sculptor Bernini. At the same time his rival Borromini was assiduously adding curve and counter-curve to the façade of San Carlo alle Quattro Fontane and to the delicate chapel of Sant'Ivo. His art offers a foretaste of the achievements of the eighteenth-century Rococo style, such as the Piazza Sant'Ignazio.

Rome as capital of Italy

The city was elevated in 1870 to a new rank – capital of a reunited Italy. Throughout the nineteenth century visitors and artists from all over the world flocked to Rome to admire the famous city. The authorities immediately launched a wave of building works including the construction of great public squares like the Piazza della Repubblica and the Piazza di Venezia, and of political and administrative buildings, as well as commemorative monuments. Rented apartment blocks spread from the Prati district, near the Castel Sant'Angelo, to Santa Maria Maggiore, quickly overrunning the ancient Aurelian Wall. In the 1930s, Rome's population passed the million mark: five times its size in 1870. Courting a place in history, Mussolini created a new district in the south, the EUR (Esposizione Universale di Roma), the completion of which was delayed by the war till the 1960s.

Since then, Rome has never ceased expanding. Hundreds of construction projects were inaugurated to mark the year 2000: innumerable palaces, churches, and gardens were restored; frescos dating from Nero's time were rediscovered; and Rome received a Millennium present – the new auditorium by Renzo Piano.

The Via del Velabro, lying between the Palatine and the Capitol, runs through one of the city's most fascinating quarters. Lined with ochre-fronted houses, it is a miniature of Roman history, where traces of the Etruscan period blend with relics of imperial times and the first centuries of Christianity.

Narrow, shadow-laden side streets and tiny squares sporting fountains huddle about the Piazza Navona –
this is Rome's most friendly face. The city remains as fascinating as ever, with its kaleidoscopic
variety of churches and palaces. Antiquity hovers discreetly in the background, a reminder,
no doubt, that in this turbulent heart of an ancient civilisation, life never stands still.

The Tiber loop

T he Neptune Fountain (Fontana del Nettuno) sparkles on the far north side of the Piazza Navona, its sculptures, full of life and grace, standing out brightly against the reddish brown façades of the solid town houses. With its basin designed by Giacomo della Porta, the fountain already existed in the sixteenth century, but had to wait some three hundred years before it received its statues.

The Corso Vittorio Emanuele II

From the Piazza di Venezia, the Via del Plebescito runs alongside the Palazzo Venezia to join the Corso Vittorio Emanuele II, a grand boulevard opened in 1870, which bisects the heart of the city before heading off towards the Vatican. At its entrance stands the Gesù (original design: 1575), the mother-church of the Jesuit Order in Rome. The building was designed by Vignola and Giacomo della Porta, and echoes in the minutest detail the ethos of the Counter-Reformation, with its profusely lit altar and its extraordinarily rich decoration. The dizzying Baroque fresco adorning the vaulting, by Baciccia, is a masterpiece of trompe-l'oeil and simulated movement, incorporating both relief work and painted surfaces.

Beyond the Largo Argentina, with its ruined classical temples and the theatre which witnessed the first production of Rossini's *Barber of Seville*, the Corso skirts the Baroque frontage of Sant'Andrea della Valle. Its dome, the work of Carlo Maderna, is surpassed in height only by that of St Peter's. Continuing further, the visitor will feel an urge to peep inside more than one *palazzo*, especially the Cancelleria, whose façade and Renaissance courtyard are the epitome of elegance.

The magnificent setting of the Piazza Navona, commissioned by Pope Innocent X (1644–1655) is the work of Bernini. A favourite meeting-place for Romans, the square can be likened to an open-air sculpture gallery, where the materials are stone and water.

The Campo dei Fiori

Accessible from the Via della Cancelleria, this square lined with tall old houses offers one of the best postcard views in Rome. It is best enjoyed in the morning, when its typically Mediterranean market is in full swing. However, in papal Rome the site was used for the execution of criminals and heretics, such as Giordano Bruno, the philosopher and theologian. Close by, the Via dei Guibbonari is a popular thoroughfare with its lively little bars and varied businesses. The wealthy families constructed their *palazzi* south of the Campo dei Fiori, nearer the Tiber. The first was the Palazzo Farnese, built during the Renaissance by Vignola and Giacomo della Porta: possibly one of the most impressive aristocratic mansions in the city. Since the reign of Louis XIII, it has served as the French Embassy. Next to it, tucked away, is the palace of Cardinal Spada, built a few years later in the purest Mannerist style, with pediments and decorative stucco garlands. Only a few steps more bring you to the Lungotevere Tebaldi and the Tiber, with a fine view towards Trastevere and the Janiculum.

ORA PRO NOBIS

The Via Giulia

The avenue behind the Palazzo Farnese is named after Pope Julius II, who hacked away tortuous alleys and medieval quarters to form one of the city's few straight thoroughfares. The new Via Giulia formed part of a direct link between the Capitol and the Vatican. Bordered with numerous churches, it was a fashionable area in the sixteenth century, when it attracted the Tuscan community, and aristocrats of every type erected their mansions there. However, in the 1700s, the construction of state prisons – the Carceri Nuove at no. 52 – put a sudden end to the street's popularity… Today, it has regained much of its charm as a district of art galleries and antique shops.

In the Fontana dei Fiumi, Bernini and his pupils personified the Rivers Danube, Ganges, Nile, and Plate, symbols respectively of Europe, Asia, Africa, and America. According to legend, the upraised arm of the allegorical River Plate represents an attempt to defend the fountain from the collapse of Sant'Agnese, the church just opposite. But Borromini's building – he was Bernini's mortal enemy – actually dates from several years later…

Facing page: Bernini's elephant with an obelisk on its back stands in front of the church Santa Maria Sopra Minerva.

Towards the Piazza Navona

The Via Giulia ends not far from the Ponte Vittorio Emanuele II. On the other side of the Corso sprawls what was once the business centre of Renaissance Rome. The Genoese and Florentine bankers installed themselves behind the Palazzo del Banco di Spirito and the Chiesa Nuova, along the Via dei Banchi Nuovi and the Via del Governo Vecchio, on the ancient route taken by the popes from the Vatican to the Lateran. The Via dei Coronari, constructed by Sixtus IV (1471–1484), marked the northern limit of this commercial area where almost the entire population of Rome was concentrated during the Renaissance; today, still lined with Renaissance palaces, the street is famous for its antique shops. As its name suggests, it was formerly the haunt of rosary-sellers who hawked religious

The Pantheon owes its survival to Pope Boniface IV (608–615), who converted it into a church and dedicated it to St Mary of the Martyrs. It contains the tombs of Raphael, Annibale Carracci, and Peruzzi, as well as of several monarchs, including Victor Emmanuel II (1861–1878), first king of the reunified Italy.
Facing page: The central oculus of the dome is the Pantheon's only source of illumination.

*F*acing page: Sant'Antonio dei Portoghesi, the national church of Rome's Portuguese community, bears the arms of the house of Braganza, which ruled Portugal from the end of the seventeenth century. The riot of gilding, stucco, and marble was financed in large part by Brazilian gold.

*T*his page: The church of Sant'Andrea della Valle, completed in the seventeenth century, plays with typical Baroque contrasts. The relatively sober nave is countered by the exuberant decoration of the choir and apse, as if to lead the eye towards a vision of divine ecstasy.

Baroque art produced a thousand variations on the construction of the dome; in the church of Sant'Ambrogio and San Carlo al Corso, the effect is one of shimmering colour.

trinkets to passing pilgrims. Beyond the Palazzo Lancelotti, a small side street leads to Santa Maria della Pace, one of whose chapels is the setting for Raphael's four Sibyls. The delightful campo is, like the façade, by the great Baroque architect Pietro da Cortona. A small café in 1900s style, always packed, adds another attractive touch. Not far from the Piazza Navona, the façade of the modest San Nicola dei Lorenesi has just been restored; the name reveals that it was once the national church of emigrants from Lorraine.

T he Column of Marcus Aurelius relates significant incidents in his Danube campaign, though Aurelius was devoted to Stoic philosophy more than to the arts of war.

The Piazza Navona

It is hard not to fall for the charm of this big square full of the sound of plashing fountains and surrounded by *palazzi* with fine, warm-coloured fronts. Its lively bustle, which never seems to slacken, lends it a magic which has captivated generations of tourists. Even the Romans never tire of it.

It should be visited early in the morning, when the sound of the water seems to echo from building to building, and again in the evening, when the place is murmurous with the voices of the crowds.

The shape of the Piazza Navona is deliberately reminiscent of Domitian's Stadium, constructed on this site in AD 86 for Greek-style athletic contests. Before housing the great Capitoline market during the Renaissance, the square long remained a heap of rubble which local inhabitants plundered to build their homes.

The stunning design of this square was the brainchild of Pope Innocent X (1644–1655), who decided soon after his election to rebuild the church of Sant'Agnese and the Palazzo Pamphili. Bernini was chosen to create the fountains which set off to perfection both the square and the pontiff's family dwelling. The finest, the Fontana dei Fiumi, has pride of place in the centre. According to legend, the statues of the Nile and the Plate are raising their arms to guard against the imminent collapse of Sant'Agnese's façade. The symbolism becomes clear when we remember that one of the architects of this church was Borromini, who was Bernini's mortal enemy.

Around the Pantheon

The heart of the ancient Campus Martius or Field of Mars was close by the Piazza Navona, in the area surrounding the Pantheon. It is still a district of small, busy side streets swarming with churches, *palazzi*, and enticing squares. Beside the Palazzo Madama, former residence of the Medici and now the home of the Senate, stands the church of San Luigi dei Francesi – literally, St Louis of the French. Completed in 1589, it is the national church for French expatriates in Rome, and its stately façade displays the salamander, emblem of Francis I. Inside are three famous paintings by Caravaggio illustrating the life of St Matthew. Not far away, make sure you visit the attractive Renaissance courtyard of the Palazzo della Sapienza. Here you will find a little jewel by the

The façade of the Palazzo Farnese gives a typical Renaissance impression of solidity and permanence. The arms of the Farnese dynasty over the monumental entrance were the work of Michelangelo. This, the largest and perhaps the most beautiful of Roman palaces, conceals countless graceful and exquisite details behind its rather austere exterior. The leading architects of the day were pressed into service to design and decorate the residence of Pope Paul III (1534–1549): first Antonio da Sangallo, then Michelangelo, and finally Giacomo della Porta.

Baroque architect Borromini: the Sant'Ivo Chapel. Leaving the maze of straight and shadowy side streets, you suddenly come out into the Piazza della Rotonda: a beautiful setting for the imposing bulk of the Pantheon. This, the best preserved of all Rome's ancient monuments, was raised by Agrippa in the first century BC; rebuilt by Hadrian (117–138), it was transformed into a church in the seventh century. The dome which crowns its geometric design is 43.30 m (142 ft) in diameter and one of the largest ever constructed. Two other important Roman churches lie close to the Pantheon. Santa Maria Sopra Minerva, the city's only Gothic building, overlooks a square with a sculpture of an elephant carrying an obelisk: one of Bernini's caprices. Further to the north, Sant'Ignazio is famous for its painted vaulting, celebrating St Ignatius of Loyola's triumphal entry to Paradise.

Piazza Montecitorio

In Antiquity, funeral pyres were built in the northern part of the Campus Martius, which was also the site of wealthy families' monuments. Like the environs of the Piazza Navona, Montecitorio was completely redesigned by that great city planner Pope Sixtus IV (1471–1484). Nowadays it has become a district of banks and large stores.

The Piazza Montecitorio is dominated by a *palazzo* in a curious mixture of Baroque and Liberty styles which houses the Chamber of Deputies. One side of the Montecitorio opens onto another square, the Piazza Colonna, among the busiest in Rome; at its centre, towering over the Corso, soars a column commemorating Marcus Aurelius. On the other side of the Montecitorio, towards the Tiber, there is a labyrinthine network of small streets preserving all the atmosphere of Renaissance Rome.

Sant'Ivo, with its concave façade and multi-faceted drum, forms the fourth side of the courtyard of the Palazzo della Sapienza. Tucked away from the public gaze, this little church is one of the nicest surprises in the vicinity of the Piazza Navona. The lantern, a minor miracle of Baroque design, is by the architect Borromini, who completed his whimsical conquest of the vertical with an elegant corkscrew spire.

Following pages: The Madonna is present everywhere in the heart of Rome, adorning the walls of palaces, the interiors of the most secretive courtyards, the corners of busy streets. As these images show, devotion to her is as strong as ever.

AVE GRATIA PLENA

VERGINE IMMACOLATA MARIA
MADRE DEL DIVINO AMORE
FATECI SANTI

The right bank of the Tiber epitomises two distinctive aspects of the city. Nearest the river, bubbling with life, and with any excuse for a celebration, lies the world of Trastevere's alleys and side streets. The tone changes on the heights of the Janiculum, with its fabulous viewpoints and its patrician mansions slumbering amongst green trees – the stuff of dreams.

Trastevere and the Janiculum

Peeling plasterwork and Vespas abandoned in the street – this is Trastevere, with its atmosphere of indifference and its love of passionate arguments. Trastevere is the real face of Rome, stripped of the pomp and show.

Trastevere

This is one of the pleasantest parts of Rome. It has become rather 'touristy', but if you stroll round the twisting little side streets you may still come across old women, all dressed in black, sitting on their doorsteps with their knitting, or groups of men playing cards. Everywhere modest houses with their lines of washing are reminders that Trastevere is indeed the 'most Roman' of all the city's districts.

The 'place over the Tiber' (the literal meaning of Trastevere) already had a reputation as a 'popular' district way back in Antiquity. It was home to small traders, artisans, and sailors attracted by the nearby port on the Tiber, as well as to a large Jewish community and Christians from the East. There were no important temples, only utilitarian buildings and little sanctuaries dedicated to obscure divinities.

After vegetating for a long while, Trastevere underwent a limited resurgence around the year 1000 before becoming Rome's thirteenth district some two hundred years later. But it was always to remain the Eternal City's poor relation. In the Baroque age, few *palazzi* were built here – it was considered sufficient to embellish the churches. This was

*T*he church of Santa Maria in Trastevere is a virtual museum of the lapidary's craft, containing the stone coffins of cardinals, engraved funerary plaques, and a whole collection of fragments from the early Christian era.

the case with those buildings close to the river bank: San Francesco a Ripa, La Madonna dell'Orto, Santa Cecilia, and San Crisogono, though the last named has retained its twelfth-century Romanesque *campanile*. Santa Maria in Trastevere, famous for its Romanesque mosaics, has preserved its medieval appearance, despite the addition of a portico in the eighteenth century. It stands at the very heart of the quarter, beside a square with a Baroque fountain – a focal point where countless little streets converge. The first religious building would have been constructed on this site at the start of the third century by Pope (later St) Calixtus (217–222), making Santa Maria Rome's earliest church.

Trastevere owes its character to its inaccessibility. In the past the district was only linked to the left bank by the Isola Tiberina, whose travertine 'prow' and an obelisk reminiscent of a mast accentuated its ship-like appearance. The Ancient Romans believed that Aesculapius had visited the island in the guise of a boat; a temple was erected there to the god of medicine, and the theme is perpetuated, as it were, by the present hospital.

Two ancient bridges, one on each side of the Isola, span the River Tiber. The Ponte Cestio (Latin: Pons Cestius) on the Trastevere side dates from 46 BC, but has been altered since. Linking the island with the east bank and the site of the medieval Jewish ghetto is the Ponte Fabricio – the Pons Fabricius, the oldest bridge in the capital (62 BC). Named after its builder, the consul Fabricius, its nickname 'Bridge of Four Heads' derives from the four-sided heads of Hermes at the far end. At the end of the fifteenth century, the construction of the Sistine Bridge (Ponte Sisto) relieved Trastevere's isolation upstream. There is a story that the pope who commissioned it, Sixtus IV, raised the necessary funds by taxing Roman prostitutes...

Statues of saints, added in the seventeenth and eighteenth centuries, set against the mosaics forming the cornice of Santa Maria in Trastevere. The Virgin with Child is depicted as a queen accompanied by her courtiers.

The Janiculum

Dominating Trastevere with its lighthouse, the hill known in ancient times as the Janiculum (modern Italian: Gianicolo), the dwelling of the god Janus, begins to rise just beyond the Ponte Cestio. On its heights, green with lawns and trees, the network of small streets gives way to villas set in their own estates and a lush botanical garden – the Orto Botanico – where orchids blossom among the sequoias and palms. The hill remained virtually in its natural state until the early Renaissance, when nobles and churchmen took it over for their sumptuous country villas.

Cardinal Domenico Riario, nephew of Pope Sixtus IV (1471–1484), was one of the first to fall under the spell of the Janiculum. He chose the site for his summer villa, which was the residence of Queen Christina of Sweden in the seventeenth century. Extensively renovated in the 1700s, the mansion then took the name of its new owner, Cardinal Corsini.

On the other side of the Via della Lungara, the Villa Farnesina was built at the very beginning of the sixteenth century by the banker and patron of the arts Agostino Chigi. Surrounded by gardens, this typical Renaissance villa was renowned throughout Europe for its magnificent receptions: even the popes deigned to accept invitations. The place teemed with artists and intellectuals, foremost among whom were Raphael, Sebastiano del Piombo, and Il Sodoma, who together created the wonderful frescos adorning the interior.

But what really sets the Janiculum apart is its height and its panoramic views over Rome. The first is from the esplanade of San Pietro in Montorio, where, according to legend, St. Peter was crucified. Not far away lies the Tempietto (1499), an architectural gem by Bramante. From there, the Passeggiata del Gianicolo or Janiculum Walk, dating from 1884, winds among the umbrella pines, finally reaching the Piazza Garibaldi, where the bird's-eye view thrilled Chateaubriand, Stendhal, and Zola.

Houses in Trastevere – the 'place across the Tiber' – are simple and solid. In the Middle Ages they were home to a large working-class community of artisans and traders.

*M*arble *takes many forms. Emperors, popes, nobles, and the bourgeoisie used it on a lavish scale to beautify Rome's temples, churches, and palaces.*

The various types include: Carrara (snow-white marble from Tuscany), brocatello *or clouded marble,* cipolin *(white with green bands: sometimes called onion marble),* griotte *(with red and brown patches),* ophite *(dark green with white steaks),* Parian *(translucent white), and* turquin, *a blue variety.*

• Marble and marble masons •

The Romans made wide use of marble from the second century BC after discovering the many architectural wonders of Greece and Asia Minor. Their passion for this precious material could never be satisfied. Claudius (AD 41–54) even employed it in the Circus Maximus to replace the original tufa of the stables. If the art of Roman marble masons was renowned during the Late Empire and early Christianity, it reached new heights of splendour in the Middle Ages under the Cosmati school, who produced liturgical furnishings for the popes, embellished the city's *campanili*, and designed elegant spiral pillars for monastery cloisters. This family of masons gave its name to the art form known as Cosmatesque; even today a few craftsmen maintain the tradition of refined geometrical shapes and polychromatic effects resembling mosaic work.

This is the Rome the whole world knows: a very different place from those little café-lined squares, those side streets inviting a gentle stroll. Since the very beginning, the Vatican has played for the highest stakes and its history has always been writ large. It is all about size, Baroque grandeur, the triumph of Christianity. And there's a real frontier, too, protected by the famous Swiss Guards, dividing the city from the Vatican.

The Castel Sant'Angelo and the Vatican

Sant'Angelo: bridge and castle

The origins of the Ponte Sant'Angelo go back to the second century, when it linked the Campus Martius on the right bank with the huge, rotunda-crowned Mausoleum of Hadrian, which in the third century was transformed into a massive fortress, today's Castel Sant'Angelo. Around 1530, Pope Clement VII (1523–1534) commissioned statues of St Peter and St Paul for the castle end of the bridge, replacing two chapels. Clement IX (1667–1669) had Bernini add ten angels in the following century. He it is, then, to whom we owe this brilliant piece of Baroque theatre – most effective seen at night – which forms part of the pilgrim route to St Peter's. The castle takes its name from a legend. In 590, Pope Gregory the Great (590–604) had a vision of the Archangel Michael sheathing his sword on top of the Mausoleum. It was taken as a sign from Heaven that the plague which had been ravaging the city was finally over. The castle's round form reflects that of the Hadrianeum. It has served countless purposes over the course of time: originally an outpost of the Aurelian Wall (fifth century), it became a refuge – and even a prison – for the medieval popes. It was to the Castel Sant'Angelo that Clement VII fled from the Vatican to escape the fury of Charles V's mercenaries, using the Passetto, a passage specially constructed

Facing page: In AD 64, after the massive fire which he had started himself, Nero ordered the executions of thousands of Christians. Peter, who was probably one of the victims, chose to be crucified head downwards in Nero's circus. He was buried at the spot where, in 326, Constantine II was to erect the first St Peter's basilica.

This page: Pope Pius IX (1846–1878), who erected the Column of the Immaculate Conception bearing figures of four Old Testament characters (Moses, Isaiah, Ezekiel, and David), was caught up in the struggle for Italian reunification in 1870. Considering himself a prisoner of the king of Italy and proclaimed the doctrine of papal infallibility.

St Peter's Square, despite its enormous size, can scarcely hold the crowds who come to catch a glimpse of the pope. Originally, Bernini wished to erect a triumphal arch between the two arms of the colonnade, which would suddenly reveal St Peter's to approaching pilgrims. Nowadays, the Via della Conciliazione offers a spectacular view towards the Basilica from the banks of the Tiber.

for such emergencies in the high linking wall. The interior, with its spiral ramp and its sumptuous Renaissance apartments, is breathtaking. Then there is the view from the summit – an all-embracing panorama of the city's hills, domes, and *campanili*.

The Prati di Castello and the Piazza Mazzini

The imposing bulk of the Palace of Justice (Palazzo di Giustizia), a Neobaroque construction dating from around 1900, offers a striking contrast with the Castel Sant'Angelo. One of the façades overloaded with allegorical statues faces the Tiber, the other gazes down on the Piazza Cavour, which marks the start of the district known as Prati di Castello. This quarter is notable for its wide streets laid out in perfectly straight lines. The apartment blocks date from 1880 onwards and were designed to house civil servants from Turin. Walking further toward the north, you can reach the Piazza Mazzini, a huge 'green' square with a large fountain, where a number of important arteries converge.

The Via della Conciliazione

This long boulevard starts at the Castel Sant'Angelo and extends to the Vatican City. Its name recalls the 'Reconciliation' following the Lateran Treaty of 1929 whereby the Vatican was raised to the status of an independent state. The alignment of the new, broad avenue, one of Mussolini's projects, involved the destruction of an old district and many palaces. Its design also obliterated the effect of surprise intended by Bernini, who had in mind the pilgrims forced to navigate a maze of side streets before suddenly emerging in front of the Basilica, in this gigantic, colonnaded square, where they must have experienced the kind of shock so dear to Baroque design. Today, the view up the Via della Conciliazione, lined at intervals with strategic viewpoints in the form of obelisks, is such that the visitor feels literally snatched towards St Peter's.

Since the pontificate of Julius II (1503–1513), successive popes have amassed a vast collection of works of art in the Vatican. Today, its museums and galleries rank among the world's finest.

This page: Popes were not alone in receiving the signal honour of being buried in St Peter's. The last Stuarts also have their tombs here, designed by the Neoclassical sculptor Antonio Canova.
Facing page: It fell to Bernini to give the finishing touches to St Peter's, work on which had started a century earlier. Symbolising the Basilica's final completion is the famous bronze Baldaquin, which succeeds in unifying the interior space.

St Peter's Square

Viewing the absolute perfection of the triumphal vestibule to St Peter's is a unique experience. Taking a liberty which was amazing at the time, Bernini substituted the curve for the right angle considered essential in the construction of the traditional *atrium* or forecourt.

Surrounded by 140 statues of saints, St Peter's Square is both a symbol of the Church extending its arms to welcome pilgrims as well as a major expression of Baroque art. Bernini, commissioned by Alexander VII (1655–1667), has created a trapezoidal space vast enough to accommodate crowds of pilgrims and allowing each to catch sight of the pontiff when he appears on the balcony of St Peter's. With a view to the pageantry of liturgical processions, Bernini also created a quadruple colonnade. Last, and of course not least, the square was designed to set off St Peter's by the use of optical illusions which make the Basilica look higher than it is.

St Peter's Basilica

In the fourth century, the Emperor Constantine (312–337) erected the first basilica on the spot where St Peter had been buried. If we believe the accounts, it was immense, and its façade glowed with mosaics. In the ninth and tenth centuries, the church served as a magnificent setting for the coronations of Holy Roman Emperors like Charlemagne, Charles the Bald, and Otto I. But by the 1300s, after a thousand years of existence, this venerable edifice stood on the verge of ruin.

Reconstruction was unavoidable. The task fell to Julius II (1503–1513) from the early 1500s. He accepted the plans drawn up by Bramante, who had conceived the idea of crowning the basilica with a dome like that of the Pantheon. Work was interrupted by the deaths of Julius and his architect, but resumed in the pontificate of Paul III (1534–1549). Michelangelo, a former pupil of Bramante, was appointed architect-in-charge. Resuming his master's design, he abandoned the idea of a flattened cupola and set to work on a huge drum that would dominate the skyline. He died in 1564, his masterpiece unfinished; it was finally completed by Giacomo della Porta and Domenico Fontana at the end of the century. But by then the Counter-Reformation was in full swing, and in church design the Latin cross had become the norm. Paul III therefore employed Carlo Maderna to

The marble masons accomplished wonders of inventiveness and skill in the decoration of St Peter's and the Vatican palaces. Clement XII (1730–1740), whose coat of arms is set in the marble floor of St. Peter's, commissioned the celebrated Trevi Fountain.

Following pages: The circular design of the Castel Sant'Angelo, which served on more than one occasion as a refuge for the popes, deliberately echoes that of Hadrian's Mausoleum. The Ponte Sant'Angelo, with its Bernini angels, replaces the bridge erected by Hadrian in the second century.

By following a passageway built into the long wall known as the Passetto – created by Alexander VI (1492–1503) – the popes were able to escape to the Castel Sant'Angelo if the Vatican came under siege.

lengthen the nave and redesign the façade, arousing lively criticism since Michelangelo's dome was now partly masked.

The Basilica was eventually consecrated on 18 November 1626, to mark the 1,300th anniversary of the consecration of Constantine's church. Bernini had only just managed to complete the famous Baldaquin, whose dizzy height and unparalleled richness of decoration distinguish the high altar where only the pope is entitled to say Mass. Later, Alexander VII (1655–1667) asked Bernini to decorate the apse. It was there that the artist placed St Peter's Chair. Above is a 'gloria' showing the triumph of the Holy Spirit in the form of a dove. Seen from the nave, the work is framed to perfection between the twisted bronze columns of the Baldaquin which Bernini had set in place some thirty years earlier. The overall effect is a stupendous Baroque paean to the glory of the Church Universal. In a few decades, Bernini had transformed the interior of St Peter's into a grandiose theatre of marble and gold. All in all, the construction of the world's largest basilica had taken more than a

century and a half. It extended over twenty or so pontificates and required the service of some ten architects.

The Vatican gardens and palace

On returning to Rome after their exile in Avignon, the popes abandoned their Lateran Palace and took up residence near St Peter's. Work began in the fifteenth century, under the pontificate of Nicholas V (1447–1455); it was continued by Sixtus IV (1471–1484), who gave his name to the Sistine Chapel, and especially by Julius II during the Renaissance. It is to this great papal builder that we owe the two most resplendent treasures of the Vatican: the ceiling of the Sistine Chapel, painted by Michelangelo, and the decoration of the Stanze and Loggia, by Raphael. The pontiffs ceaselessly improved their palaces right up to the end of the nineteenth century; taking their cue from Julius II, they acquired a huge quantity of *objets d'art* for the Vatican, in what has become a unique collection. Vatican City, the world's smallest state (roughly 44 hectares or 109 acres) is now home to some ten museums or galleries covering every aspect of human

An unexpected face of Rome: the area around the Piazza Mazzini, green and relaxed. The only link between the rest of Rome and this nineteenth-century district is a splendid fountain in the great Baroque tradition.

The Palace of Justice (Palazzo di Giustizia, 1889–1910), just beside the Castel Sant'Angelo, remains among the most impressive public buildings of modern Rome. The nineteenth century adored allegory. The visitor passes through a courtyard amongst figures of the great jurists, including Cicero himself, finally entering through the monumental doorway surmounted by a group representing Justice flanked by Law and Force.

knowledge and achievement. There are paintings by the Italian Primitives and the best Renaissance artists, but also masterpieces of ancient sculpture, Egyptian and Etruscan art, gold and silver work, tapestry, and Greek pottery, together with ancient maps, and even collections of carriages and candelabra. But all the rest of the Vatican's inexhaustible wealth is eclipsed by two undisputed masterpieces: the Stanze of Raphael and, even more famous, the Sistine Chapel. On the walls along both sides, the most talented Renaissance artists – Botticelli, Perugino, Pinturicchio, Ghirlandaio, and Luca Signorelli – prepared the way for Michelangelo, whose immortal fresco of the Last Judgement put the finishing touches to the chapel twenty years after he had painted the vault.

After such a parade of magnificence, a visit to the Vatican gardens comes as something of a relief…. There is more to these gardens, though, than a respite from the crowds. They are quite simply full of poetry and very moving: it is a little-known fact of history that the Vatican gardens were

The Piazza del Quirinale is the epitome of Roman elegance: obelisks, stately ochre façades, and ancient statues, not to mention the inevitable fountain. The Quirinal Palace (Palazzo del Quirinale), the work of the best sculptors of the sixteenth and seventeenth centuries – Domenico Fontana, Carlo Maderna, and of course the famous Bernini – is now the residence of the President of the Republic. Fronting the building is the Via del Quirinale, lined by some of the finest Roman Baroque churches, some designed by Bernini (Sant'Andrea al Quirinale), others by Borromini, Bernini's mortal enemy (San Carlo alle Quattro Fontane). This street leads to one of the glories of Baroque urban design, the Piazza delle Quattro Fontane, constructed to open up a view of Santa Maria Maggiore and the obelisks of the Trinità dei Monti.

The Piazza di Campidoglio, Rome's only remaining example of Renaissance city planning, was the work of the era's most illustrious artist, Michelangelo, who designed the Palazzo Senatorio and the steps flanked by the twin Dioscuri. Facing page: Rome owes much to Trajan (98–117), who carried out vast building programmes after seizing the gold mines in Dacia. He constructed baths and a huge forum with associated libraries and markets, as well as the famous Trajan's Column, originally crowned by his statue.

*D*espite its severe seventeenth-century façade, San Silvestro in Capite is a medieval foundation (752–757), as can be seen from its slender campanile and its atrium. The name 'Capite' (head) derives from a precious relic kept in the church: the head of St John the Baptist.

*F*ollowing pages: Santa Maria Maggiore has a seventeenth- and eighteenth-century exterior, but is in fact one of the best preserved of Rome's early Christian basilicas. The central nave, the apse, and the triumphal arch are smothered in mosaics from the time of Pope Sixtus III (432–440), who erected this church to the glory of the Virgin Mary.

*T*he Piazza della Repubblica has come to symbolise the 'New Rome' and the extraordinary change which the city underwent in the immediate aftermath of Italian reunification. The circular piazza is now a perpetual sea of traffic which sweeps around the island-like Fontana dei Naiadi (added in 1885).

Around the Piazza della Repubblica

East of the Quirinal, the atmosphere changes completely. Here the visitor discovers a city born in the aftermath of reunification, a city of big squares and avenues lined with plane trees, like the very chic Via Veneto. The Piazza della Repubblica, with its colonnaded, Neoclassical buildings, passes for the most significant achievement of nineteenth-century Roman landscaping. Nearby, the less aristocratic districts around the station and Santa Maria Maggiore equally demonstrate the extraordinary vitality of the Italian capital in the years following reunification and in the early twentieth century: you need only look at the long rows of perfectly straight streets and all those identical four- or five-storeyed buildings.

The Piazza di Venezia

Leading from the Piazza della Repubblica to the noisy Piazza Venezia is the Via Nazionale, where Rome's smart set do their shopping. Largely revamped in the nineteenth century, the Piazza Venezia is the square where Mussolini made his speeches, and one of Rome's largest road junctions. It is also the point of departure for mass demonstrations. Inevitably, the eye is drawn to the Vittoriano. Inaugurated in 1911, this huge, grandiloquent building is dedicated to Victor Emmanuel II, the first king of the reunified Italy. It has earned a number of unflattering nicknames: the 'wedding cake' and the 'typewriter', in particular.

The Capitol

Away from the uproar of the buzzing Piazza di Venezia, Rome's smallest hill appears as an oasis of Roman tranquillity. In ancient times, during the Roman Republic, it was a religious centre dominated by two temples and connecting with the Forum. The Capitol retained an important role

*R*ome is remarkable for the number of its fountains. They are to be found everywhere at street corners, often simple and almost anonymous. Others boast striking sculpted groups like Bernini's Triton or the 'Moses' Fountain – a Renaissance work by Domenico Fontana, which grandly signals the end of the Felice Aqueduct.

*With its palatial backdrop, the Trevi Fountain
is a late Baroque extravaganza. The scene immortalised in
stone recalls the passionate love of theatre and mythology
which has always characterised the Romans.*

• The Trevi Fountain •

That memorable scene in Fellini's *Il Dolce Vita* (1960) where the curvaceous Anita Ekberg takes a dip
in the Trevi would doubtless have lost its magic and eroticism had it been filmed in the modest
fountain of Nicholas V (1447–1455)… The monumental Trevi, into which thousands of tourists throw
coins (over the shoulder, looking away) and make a wish to see Rome again, was the work of Nicolò
Salvi (1732–1751). The name refers not to the Umbrian town but to the fountain's position at the
junction of *tre vie*, three streets. Salvi did not skimp on allegory: Ocean, riding a chariot drawn by
Tritons and seahorses, is flanked in the background by statues of Salubrity and Abundance. Today, the
late Baroque fountain is protected against its two main enemies – not the tourists, but lime scale and
pigeons – thanks to a water purification system and a low-voltage electric field.

The Palazzo Barberini, not far from the Via Veneto, was a joint design by the three leading exponents of Roman Baroque: Carlo Maderna, Borromini, and Bernini. Today it is the site of an art gallery whose star exhibit is the portrait of 'La Fornarina', one of Raphael's finest achievements.

throughout the Middle Ages, when it was home to the city's Senate; today, it is still the site of most municipal offices.

On the occasion of a visit by Charles V in 1536, Pope Paul III (1534–1549) ordered Michelangelo to refurbish the Piazza del Campidoglio. The artist responded by creating a subtle design to set off the senatorial palace. It included the stairway with its flanking statues of Castor and Pollux as well as the *palazzi* dominated by the silhouette of Santa Maria d'Aracoeli. The geometric paving was also part of his original design. Curiously, it lends impact to the equestrian statue of Marcus Aurelius, an emperor who despised Christianity; indeed, it was believed in the sixteenth century that the statue was of Constantine, the Christians' champion.

The most important remains of Ancient Rome are to be found here, extending as far as the eye can see between the massive white bulk of the Vittoriano and the Colosseum. Here, in a jumble of all the centuries, arches, baths, temples, and forums invite the visitor to explore the heart of a civilisation slowly re-emerging into the light of day.

From the forums to the Colosseum

The Via Sacra, the triumphal route which leads through the forum to the Temple of Jupiter on the Capitol. How many victorious generals must have driven along this way!

The Forum Romanum

This was the political, administrative, and religious centre of Rome in the days of the kings and the Republic. Around the triumphal Via Sacra, where generals paraded after successful campaigns, were ranged the city's most important monuments: the Forum and the home of the senate – the Curia – as well as a plethora of temples, basilicas, and triumphal arches.

In the beginning, however, the locality was hardly hospitable: it was a marsh which also served as a burial ground. In the sixth century BC the Etruscan king Tarquin the Elder (ca. 616– ca. 578 BC) drained the water into the Tiber, and the plain soon became the site of the city's first forum. The advent of the Republic witnessed the addition of further buildings, shops, and of course temples: one dedicated to Saturn, another to Castor and Pollux. The forum underwent continual facelifts, notably when it was lined with colonnades in the second century BC. At this time, work began on the Basilica Aemilia and the Basilica Julia, vast roofed structures divided into several 'naves' and used to transact all kinds of business. None the less, they could not compensate for the restricted size of the forum or satisfy the requirements of a million or so inhabitants. Activity then began to extend towards the Campus Martius, in the area around the Pantheon, and, a little further north, to the new imperial forums. By depriving it of its essential

The Arch of Constantine stands a stone's throw from the Colosseum. Its prolific decoration was created by robbing other monuments, to the extent that Marcus Aurelius appears as often as the founder of Constantinople…

functions, the emperors were to transform the heart of Rome's economic power into a stage for their own glorification. They accelerated this change by adding commemorative or religious monuments. Augustus (27 BC–AD 14), Titus (79–81), and Septimius Severus (193–211) raised triumphal arches; Antoninus Pius (138–161), Maxentius (306–312), and Constantine (312–337) built new temples.

Today, an air of desolation broods over the ruin-strewn wasteland that was the Forum Romanum. Here and there emerge the elegant Corinthian columns of the Temple of Castor and Pollux, part of a colonnade, and the series of statues which graced the House of the Vestals (Atrium Vestae). Further off, the arcades of the Basilica of Maxentius and Constantine bear witness to the last flowering of an empire in decline. The most evocative ruins are the triumphal arches on either side of the Via Sacra. Near the brick building which housed the Curia, that of Septimius Severus (203 AD) is remarkable for its extravagant decoration, while the slender first-century Arch of Titus still seems to be watching over the 'grandeur that was Rome'.

The imperial forums

In the first century BC, Julius Caesar (d. 44 BC) decided to construct a new

forum north of the old one. Four emperors followed his example: first

Augustus (27 BC–AD 14), then Vespasian (69–79), Nerva (96–98), and

Trajan (98–117) each built a forum on one side or the other of the present

Via dei Fori Imperiali, striving to outdo one another in magnificence,

raising colonnades, libraries, and basilicas – each more sumptuous than

their predecessors', and all in a profusion of marble. In less than a century a

new city was born, its wealth reflecting the golden age of imperial Rome.

Trajan produced the most impressive of the forums, and the best preserved

today: the Forum Trajanum. Work on the chosen site involved the levelling

of a plain and the cutting back of a spur of the Quirinal, all at enormous

expense. But Trajan had no need to count the cost: the plunder brought

back from his victorious campaigns in Dacia (present-day Romania)

financed the entire complex. His market, comprising 150 shops, dominated

the forum: the complex was concave in shape and occupied terraces cut into

The ruins of the Forum Romanum and the Forum Julium, once the heart of an empire which ruled the world. Now the umbrella pines keep silent vigil…

the hillside. We must leave to the imagination the riot of marble porticoes and effigies of famous Roman statesmen surrounding Trajan's equestrian statue – in gilt bronze – which took pride of place in the centre of the forum. At the other side of the square, his column still thrusts skywards, one of Ancient Rome's most familiar symbols. The seventeen Carrara marble drums, sculpted into continuous spiral panels, recount the conquest of the Dacians.

The Palatine

Mantled with spreading trees and umbrella pines since the Renaissance, this hill is the cradle of Rome. According to legend, it was the home of Romulus. Colonised by early settlers from the Aegean, the Palatine became, during Republican days, the first choice for the mansions of the Roman nobility. Then Augustus built a residence there; his successors followed suit, hence the name Palatine, from the Latin *palatium*: palace.

The Palace of Domitian is a vast complex, almost totally in ruins today. Symbolically, it was aligned south-east, that is, towards the provinces of the

Orient, the principal sources of Rome's wealth. From the Domus Augustana, their official residence, the emperors and their families could watch the games in the stadium built by Domitian, emperor from AD 81 to 96.

The Circus Maximus and environs

Now transformed into a long esplanade, the valley separating the Palatine from the Aventine was an ideal place to construct a large circus. The Circus Maximus dates from around the fourth century BC, but was constantly enlarged by the emperors; one lap of the U-shaped track was – depending on the period – about 1,500 m (1,640 yds) and the races involved chariots drawn by two, three, or four horses. The number of spectators who could be accommodated has been variously calculated at somewhere between 150,000 and 385,000.

The plain lying at the extremity of the Circus, in the direction of the Tiber, has always been an important commercial area. The district took on a fresh lease of life in the Middle Ages when it was home to a large population of

Trajan's forum, at the foot of the Quirinal, was the grandest of the imperial forums, its extravaganza of colonnades, basilicas, and porticoes evidence of a civilisation at its height.

artisans and foreign merchants. Though the architectural face of the Circus was transformed by Baroque and later developments, the extraordinary density of churches sited close to the Roman remains testifies to its importance in the city's history.

Santa Maria in Cosmedin, whose *campanile* towers over the Piazza della Bocca della Verità, is the district's finest building. Of ancient foundation (seventh century) like most of the churches near the Tiber, it was the national church of Rome's Greek community: the name, 'Cosmedin', refers to a district in Byzantium, later Constantinople.

The Aventine

Ancient Rome's southernmost hill was originally home to the plebeians. Under the Empire, the character of the Aventine changed, and it became a desirable residential area for the rest of the city's history. Today, it is a peaceful neighbourhood, green and praised for its gardens. One of these, the Giardino Savello, planted with orange trees, umbrella pines, cypresses, and laurels,

Facing page: On the slopes of the Palatine, close by the Tiber, the Arch of Janus rubs shoulders with the early church of San Giorgio in Velabro, whose bell tower was added in the 1100s.
This page, left: Beside the Piazza della Bocca della Verità, also near the Tiber, soars the gracious campanile *of Santa Maria in Cosmedin, the Greek national church in Rome. Not far off, the guild of money-changers erected the so-called Arco degli Argenteri, in reality an arch in honour of the emperor Septimius Severus. (Detail: top right.)*
Preceding pages: The Forum Romanum, originally marshland. This unpromising site, thanks to the united efforts and determination of the Romans, became first the city's business centre, then the heart of its religious activity, as is recalled by the eight columns of the Temple of Saturn (left).

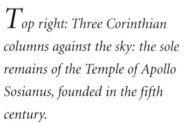

*T*op right: Three Corinthian columns against the sky: the sole remains of the Temple of Apollo Sosianus, founded in the fifth century.

Facing page: The curious spectacle of the Ponte Rotto – the Broken Bridge – one of whose spans is stranded in the middle of the Tiber downstream from the Isola Tiberina. The bridge collapsed at least twice before its reconstruction by Gregory XIII in 1575, and again in 1598.

BINEA.SQVISVNINPINGS.BER
VP.III.SEVALIAS.V.BERSVB.E
VBA.RIGS.QVISVNTINFVNDAT
ANI.CVMCASIS.ETBIN.SIMVLV
BERSVR.INSSTOFVND.QVODDA
TA.SVNTABEREDIB.GERMANA
MEAEMOLA.QVEM.DATA.EST
ABERED.PAVLI.IVXTAEAD.DV
III.VNCIAS.MOLAE.QVIDATAE
BINEASTABVL.XI.QVISVNTIA
ACEITBINEASTABVLIIS.QVISV
NTESTACIONECNONTABVL.XVIIIQ
SVNTINSCOGORDIANO.NECNON
TABVLASII.QSVNTINSCOE
VPLVM.DEBERODIPTIC.PE
QVIPROTEMPFVERIT.FACI
QVODTIDIANA.MISSACOTAP
TRESOLID.IIII.ETSIQVISPRES
VMPSERTAMDEHISLOCSO
AEAMEOFFERTASVNTETOR
DINATABELACTERISXRIANI
OBLATASVNTBELINPOSMOD

OFFERTAFVERINTABVSV
ETPOTESTAEHVIVSSCEDIAC
ALIENAREAVMONITZIONEM
EXINDECVIQVAMFACERE
SCIATSEDISTRICTVSRA
TZIONESREDDITVRVM·
ESSE·EIDEMDEI·GENETRI
CIS·INFVTVROIVDICOINSVP
ERACTANATHEMATISBINCVLO
SITINNODATVSETAREGNODI
ALIENVS·ATQVECVMDIABVLO
ETOMHIBVSINPIIS·AETERN
IO·INCENDIO·DEPVTATVS

offers an enchanting view over the city. Churches and monasteries were quick to sprout on the Aventine. Santa Sabina has kept its early Christian atmosphere despite restorations. Another church, Sant'Alessio, with its Romanesque bell tower, can be found not far from the Piazza dei Cavalieri di Malta, which is one of the few architectural designs left by Piranesi.

The Colosseum and the Arch of Constantine

Everyone recognises the Colosseum with its three tiers of arcading. Strangely, it was not until the first century after Christ that Rome decided on the luxury of a permanent amphitheatre for its infamous blood sports. Completed under Titus, the arena is in the form of an ellipse measuring 190 by 155 m (620 by 513 ft) overall. Some 50,000 spectators could be accommodated to watch the gladiators and wild beast shows, protected

In the porch of Santa Maria in Cosmedin stands the famous 'Bocca della Verità' (Mouth of Truth), in reality merely a cover from an ancient drain or well. According to legend, its open mouth will bite the hands of liars…
Facing page: Also in the porch is the tomb of Cardinal Alfano, chamberlain to Pope Calixtus II, who restored the church in the twelfth century.

This and facing page: The construction of street chapels and churches continued right up to the nineteenth and twentieth centuries. Their decoration draws on past styles or a somewhat affected Sulpician imagery. The areas around the Palatine and the Circus Maximus swarm with small, little-known churches whose origins are lost in the mists of time.

Overleaf: The Milvian Bridge (Ponte Milvio) recalls the conversion of Constantine and his battle against Maxentius in 312. The night before, Christ appeared to Constantine in a dream, promising him victory if he fought beneath the banner of the Cross.

from the rain or the scorching sun by the *velum* or *velarium*, a huge sailcloth awning stretched above the terraces. The games were the constant talk of Rome; the inaugural performances lasted for 100 days and involved the slaughter of over 5,000 wild animals. The arena could also be flooded for the staging of mock naval combats.

But was the Colosseum also the scene of Christian martyrdoms? Nowadays the idea is viewed with some scepticism, though the Stations of the Cross set up round the arena perpetuate the belief. Whatever the truth, gladiator shows were held here till they were banned by Honorius (395–423) in 404. Transformed into a fortress in the Middle Ages, the building soon began to serve as a stone quarry. The Arch of Constantine is scarcely less famous than its world-renowned neighbour, it was raised in 315 to commemorate the victory of Constantine over his rival Maxentius.

COEMETERIVM

Aficionados of the Middle Ages will be particularly acquainted with the Caelian Hill and the Lateran district, beyond the Colosseum. Both invite the visitor to take a thrilling journey back to the early days of Christianity; one enjoys a kind of provincial charm, the other is the authentic and popular face of Rome.

The Caelian and the Lateran

Nothing was too grand to honour the memory of Victor Emmanuel II, who freed Italy from Austrian domination. The erection of the Vittoriano, a gigantic monument to the glory of king and country, involved the obliteration of a large area of Ancient Roman remains.

The Caelian

The Caelian Hill, the largest of the seven, has formed part of the city since the seventh century BC. This popular suburb began to bristle with rented apartment blocks (Latin: *insulae*) after the Great Fire in AD 64 supposedly started by Nero (54–68). Devastated by the Normans under Robert Guiscard at the start of the Middle Ages, it was abandoned by its inhabitants, who migrated to the banks of the Tiber. The Caelian remained a stretch of countryside at the gates of Rome until the nineteenth century. Today, with its vegetable gardens and churches, the hill resembles a piece of the provinces misplaced inside the city.

In Antiquity, processions took the Via Triumphalis to the Colosseum, from where they continued to the forums in the city's heart. Near this street stood the family house of Gregory the Great (590–604), who turned the building into a convent dedicated to St. Andrea. The site is now occupied by the church of San Gregorio Magno with its wide stairway. Not far off, on a quiet square, is the impressive basilica Santi Giovanni e Paolo, commissioned by senators in the fourth century and consecrated to the martyrs St. John and St. Paul. Its fine bell tower, porch and modest

colonnade are twelfth century, while the interior was decorated from 1725–1734. Go down the steps at the west end of the right aisle to see the house said to have belonged to John and Paul, with its frescos which transport the visitor back to the dawn of Christianity.

On the way to San Clemente will be found a number of other very old churches. First is Santa Maria in Domenica (ninth century), with its almost rural charm; then Santo Stefano Rotondo (fifth century), whose circular design takes its inspiration from the Church of the Holy Sepulchre in Jerusalem.

Finally, San Clemente itself comes into view beside the Via dei Querceti. Founded in the fourth century, it is one of Rome's most ancient Christian basilicas. Though the original building was destroyed by the Normans, the Upper Basilica (twelfth century), with its two-aisled nave preceded by a porch and an *atrium*, has retained the typical early Christian layout. The apse is a mass of dazzling Romanesque mosaics depicting the Triumph of the Cross, whilst the St Catherine Chapel is decorated with frescos by the

Florentine Masolino da Panicale. The Lower Basilica corresponds to the original fourth-century foundation, and contains extremely rare frescos from the Carolingian period (eighth–ninth centuries) illustrating the life of St Clement. Yet another level lies beneath this one, housing the remains of two Roman constructions. One of them, the Mithraeum (second–third centuries), is dedicated to Mithras, an oriental divinity whose mystery cult enjoyed popularity under the Empire.

The church of the Santi Quattro Coronati, founded in the fourth century, is reached down the Via San Giovanni Laterano. Restored around 1100, the building was transformed into a fortress in the thirteenth century to protect the nearby papal palace (the Lateran) and provide a refuge for the popes in case of attack. It is a little island of calm, set amid green trees, and its exquisite thirteenth-century Benedictine cloister is a minor masterpiece in marble.

In typical medieval style, the delicately sculptured cornice harbours a whole gallery of monsters and figures with contorted faces – outcasts from the kingdom of the righteous.

The Lateran

The visitor strolling along the Via di San Giovanni in Laterano will be aware of the decidedly popular aspect of this part of Rome. After all, one of the city's most lively 'rag trade' markets is held in the Via Sannio, behind the great Basilica and the Wall of Aurelius. And it was in the grand square that the huge Communist demonstrations took place before the collapse of the Iron Curtain…

None the less, the Lateran, dominated by the massive Basilica of St John, has been the traditional territory of the popes. The district owes its name to a rich Roman family, the Laterani, who owned property here. At the beginning of the fourth century, the Emperor Constantine (312–337) founded the first basilica dedicated to St John, shortly after his victory over Maxentius. He also constructed a palace which he gave to Pope Melchiades (311–314) for the establishment of Rome's first episcopal see. It was from this seminal act in the history of Christianity that the Basilica acquired its status as the Mother Church, first among all others both in Rome and throughout the world.

The palace and church of the Lateran were the object of constant improvements, notably for Charlemagne's coronation in 800. The district saw its finest days in the 1100s, when the need to accommodate the clergy led to the construction of numerous dwelling houses. On returning from Avignon in 1377, however, Gregory XI (1370–1378) found his palace burned to the ground. He chose thereafter to live in the Vatican. From that moment, the Lateran lost its pre-eminence and its role as the centre of Christianity. The present building was reconstructed by Domenico Fontana in 1586. It was in this somewhat chilly residence that the Lateran Treaty was signed in 1929, giving the pontiffs sovereignty over Vatican City and several 'extraterritorial' properties – particularly the four 'major' basilicas of Santa Maria Maggiore, San

The Basilica of St John Lateran is the Pope's episcopal church. In the Middle Ages, John the Baptist and John the Evangelist were named as its patron saints and their statues appear on the glorious late baroque façade. Until their exile in Avignon, the popes constantly enhanced the church. After their return to Rome, they laboured to make St John Lateran a spectacular legacy of their occupation.

Facing page: The thirteenth-century cloister in the left outer aisle is a masterpiece of the Vassalletti family.

Following pages: The interior of the Basilica abounds in stucco, polychrome marbles, frescos, and mosaics, a felicitous blend of styles and periods.

Paolo fuori le mura, St Peter's, and St John Lateran – as well as the summer

villa at Castel Gandolfo among the Castelli Romani.

St John Lateran has suffered a number of disasters. Devastated by the

Vandals in the fifth century, toppled by an earthquake at the end of the ninth,

and then seriously damaged by the fire of 1308 which consumed the Lateran

Palace, it was rebuilt on each occasion. More than a score of popes worked

tirelessly to restore this highly symbolic monument where innumerable

councils were held during the Middle Ages. The building's present

appearance results primarily from the reconstruction carried out in the

Baroque period and the eighteenth century, when the façade was completed.

The Renaissance ceiling apart, the theatrical nave bears the stamp of

Borromini, whilst the transept is a fine example of the Mannerist style. The

Baptistery was also largely restored in the seventeenth century; in the time of

Constantine, this was the site of all Christian baptisms in the city.

Despite its humble exterior, the Basilica of San Clemente, more than any other building, evokes the splendour of medieval Rome in the dazzling colours of its marble paving and its twelfth-century mosaics.

Leaving Rome by the Porta Appia (now the Porta San Sebastiano), beyond the Palatine and the Baths of Caracalla, the 'Queen of Roads' headed south before finally swinging towards Brundisium (modern Brindisi), the 'Gateway to the East', on the shores of the Adriatic. It was along this road lined with umbrella pines and cypresses that generations of Ancient Romans and Christians laid their dead to rest.

The Via Appia Antica

The Via Appia is a romantic place to take a walk. It is lined with monuments, their inscriptions worn by time, and with the crumbling tombs of the great Roman families. One, the round mausoleum of Caecilia Matella, was so large that it was transformed into a medieval prison.

An ancient necropolis

The ancient Via Appia derived its name from the censor Appius Claudius, who oversaw its opening in 312 BC. In ancient times, it was lined with tombs for a considerable distance. By law, all interments had to take place outside the city, that is beyond the outer fortifications. Burial customs changed with the centuries. Under the Republic, cremation was the rule, which explains the number of *colombaria* where funerary urns were stored in public view. During imperial times, inhumation replaced the pyre. Lack of space meant that tombs had to be constructed deep in the earth – hence the catacombs. From the third century, these were reserved in the main for Christians.

The catacombs

Originally private cemeteries, the catacombs quickly became places of devotion. They were all built on more or less the same pattern, with chambers radiating from the *hypogeum* or tomb of a rich Roman family which had adopted Christianity. Converts did not come here to escape persecutions, but to honour the memory of the dead. As Christianity

spread and the number of its followers increased, the catacombs were gradually forgotten and abandoned. Those of St Calixtus and Domitilla are some distance off the Via Appia. The first owes its name to Pope Calixtus (217–222). It consists of four storeys, and the galleries extend for a considerable distance. The catacombs of Domitilla are even larger, and contain a series of frescos from the third and fourth centuries. Further on, the Via Appia descends through a valley, passing further catacombs which include the tomb of St Sebastian, martyred under Diocletian (284–305). In the subterranean chambers are graffiti of incalculable historical value invoking St Peter and St Paul, as well as paintings and stucco work.

Following pages: Numerous legends are associated with the Isola Tiberina, for instance that it was formed in the sixth century BC when the peasants who cultivated the Campus Martius hurled their corn harvest into the Tiber in protest against the expulsion of Tarquin the Proud, their king.

Until 1870, when Rome became the capital of Italy, travellers could follow the Via Ostiense through unspoilt countryside to the sea and scarcely meet a living soul. The church of San Paolo fuori le mura, which houses the tomb of St Paul, was practically the only oasis of civilisation. The late nineteenth century brought a sudden change with the development of the Testaccio district adjacent to the Aventine, while in the 1930s, Mussolini dreamed of resurrecting the glory of the Caesars in another southern suburb…

The southern suburbs

T he Palazzo della Civiltà del Lavoro designed by Guerrini, La Padula, and Romano, with its series of utterly stark colonnades. The allegorical statues of the arts on the ground floor accentuate the building's sense of immobility.

EUR

This district, to the south of Rome along the Via Ostiense, was officially born in 1937. Mussolini's *Fascisti* dreamed of celebrating the triumph of the party with a universal exposition staged in the capital in 1942 – the twentieth anniversary of the March on Rome. The war, however, interrupted their plans.

The construction of the EUR (Esposizione Universale di Roma, also known as E 42) was entrusted to the architect Marcello Piacentini and began in 1939. Two years later work was abandoned, leaving only the outline of the 'New Rome' which was to have epitomised the power of Fascism. The project was resumed in the 1950s with the construction of further buildings. At the same time, the provision of accommodation breathed a little life and humanity into the area.

The EUR, with its colossal white buildings, its vast perspectives, its silent squares, and its juxtaposition of the overwhelming and the absurd, evokes the world of the artist Giorgio de Chirico (1888–1978). The Palazzo della Civiltà del Lavoro (1938), dedicated to a favourite Fascist concept, the 'civilisation of work' – also known by the nicknames of